THE ARCHIVES

OF

BALLIOL COLLEGE

OXFORD

HENRY SAVAGE

Drawn by Alvin Ferris from the contemporary portrait which hangs in the College Hall.

The ARCHIVES of BALLIOL COLLEGE OXFORD

A GUIDE

John Jones

Dean and Archivist

PHILLIMORE

1984

Published by
PHILLIMORE & CO. LTD.
Shopwyke Hall, Chichester, Sussex

ISBN 0 85033 533 7

Printed and bound in Great Britain by
BILLINGS BOOK PLAN
Worcester, England

TO PAT

CONTENTS

I INTRODUCTION

About 1260, or perhaps a few years before, John de Balliol, the powerful Lord of Barnard Castle, was involved in a territorial dispute with the Bishop of Durham. Balliol, impatient, insulted the Bishop, who imposed a penance on him. According to the Chroniclers, he had to submit to a public whipping at Durham Cathedral door and he was also required to carry out a substantial act of charity. This he did by renting a house just outside the Oxford town wall and maintaining in it some poor scholars to whom he paid a dole of a few pence a week. The house stood roughly where the present Master's Lodgings are, looking across Horsemonger Street (now Broad Street) and the ditch or moat to the wall. The date of this foundation is traditionally reckoned as 1263. There is actually no evidence for such precision, but we do know that the little society John Balliol initiated was in existence by June 1266, when its dependence on him is mentioned in a royal writ. Whatever the exact date, if the age of a college is to be computed from the date when its members first lived communally on its present site, then Balliol is the oldest in the University.[1]

It is therefore a matter for special regret that the College is alone among the ancient foundations in having practically no direct records of its affairs in mediaeval times. Muniments establishing corporate integrity and title to property survive in abundance from the thirteenth century but registers of members, accounts and the like do not begin until about 1540, when the office of Secretary was created: internal administrative records are progressively more copious thereafter. The ancient deeds are mostly in excellent condition. It is obvious from their appearance that they were folded into small packets and carefully stored in a secure place. From the sixteenth century this place was the Vestry of the Chapel (rebuilt ca. 1530), which also served as a Treasury: it remained the Muniment Room until the nineteenth century. Of the arrangements before 1530 we know nothing, but can conjecture that the Chest which is mentioned several times between 1540 and 1580 had been long in use, probably standing in the Chapel. Movements of documents in and out of it were occasions for formality, which was carefully recorded in the Latin Register, as in the following examples:[2]

> Memorandum. That I, William Francis, in the presence of all the Fellows, took from the Chest fifty instruments concerning Abbotsley, on the 2nd day of the month of November, in the year of our Lord 1542. Item. At another time twelve court rolls concerning the same.

> Memorandum. That all the above-mentioned instruments were replaced in the Chest of the Society, on the 4th day of the following February, in the presence of the Fellows.
>
> On the 16th day of the month of January in the year of our Lord 1556, the Venerable Mr. William Wright, STB, previously (viz. on the 1st day of December immediately preceding) elected Master or Warden of Balliol College, personally laid before the Fellows, who had been convened in the Chapel of the aforesaid College, an instrument or certificate of his admission by the Bishop of Lincoln, Visitor of the aforesaid College, sealed with the seal of the Public Notary. Which instrument, when they had inspected it and heard it read, the aforesaid Fellows of the aforesaid College took in a proper manner, and placed for preservation in the College Public Chest. All of which was done lawfully, and in accordance with the meaning and form of the Statutes of the College aforesaid, on the day and year aforesaid, at about six in the afternoon.

A hundred years later the same care was still being exercised, and there was a separate Treasury Book recording deposits and withdrawals of documents as well as cash. The accumulated records were by now much more extensive and we hear of arrangements in various boxes, e.g.:[4]

> 11 Dec. 1637. Taken out of the Treasurie one double box of writings by the Vicegerent and the Society at a generall meeting ....
> 19 Jul. 1639 Taken out then, out of St. Lawrence Box one indenture to Shrawby of our houses in London. Allsoe eight other writings out of the old chests concerning Clerkenwell. The wch were by the fellows brought to the Master the same day.

After the Restoration, there was a flurry of activity among the College records. This was partly a product of the antiquarian enthusiasm of the time, but Anthony Wood was at the centre of it. The Treasury Book records that on 20 Sept. 1665 a box was "taken out of the Treasurie, To the Master's Lodgings, for the use of Mr. Anthony Wood of Merton College", and he wrote in his diary[5] that on the following day he

> began to peruse the evidences of Ball. Coll. They were taken out of the treasury there, which is a kind of vestry joyning on the south side to the east end of the chappell. The evidences were taken thence by Dr. Savage the master of that College, and conveyed to his lodgings, where A.W. perused them in a space of 3 or 4 days. The old accompts of that Coll., wherein their fellowes are either weekly or quarterly mentioned are lost. So A.W. was much put to a push to find when learned men had been of that coll.

Savage himself was also at work, publishing in 1668 'Balliofergus, or a Commentary upon the Foundation, Founders and Affaires of Balliol Colledge, Gathered out of the Records thereof, and other Antiquities. With a brief Description of Eminent Persons who have been formerly of the same House'. Balliofergus was the earliest of all College Histories, but its purpose was probably not solely historical: there is much harping on financial difficulties and past dealings in which the College had been unfairly treated. The extensive transcriptions and analyses undertaken by Nicholas Crouch (Fellow 1640-1690) were also in part motivated by concern over the College's near bankruptcy, and the need to take a more business-like attitude to the collection of debts and the administration of College estates. All this industry either exposed or created disorder, which was remedied by "Mr Willm Ball, one of the yeomen Beadles of the University". He was allowed to renew the lease of his house nearby for only half the normal fine on 29 Sept 1675, as he had "then lately been very serviceable to the Colledge, in Looking = over all the Colledge = writings in the Treasury, and Digesting them (which before, were very much Confused, and out of order) into their severall places or Boxes, to which they did properly Belong."[6] The same William Ball - an early professional archivist - performed a similar service for New College.[7]

The order reestablished by Ball prevailed, despite growth, until the mid-nineteenth century: to judge by surviving lists and endorsements in their hands, Joseph Sanford (Fellow 1714-1774), John Parsons (Master 1798-1819), Richard Jenkyns (Master 1819-1854) and Henry Wall (Fellow 1839-1871) deserve most of the credit for this. Between 1850 and 1870, however, there were extensive rebuilding works and the Archives had to be rehoused. There was some scattering, and it is probable that a good deal of bulky material was consigned to cellars at this time, soon to be forgotten. When H.T. Riley surveyed the records of the College for the Royal Commission on Historical Manuscripts in 1874,[8] he was ridiculously misled and reported that "The records of this College, in the shape of volumes, seem to be but very few in number" whereas, as the sequel describes, there were in fact several hundred volumes on the premises somewhere. He only noted one Bursars' Book, which had probably survived oblivion by being kept in the Bursary because it contained lists of plate. On 19 June 1877 a College Meeting resolved "that Mr Parker should be employed in arranging the College Papers". George Parker was a member of the Bodleian Library staff: his prodigious spare time task in Balliol was not completed until June 1889. He made a minute examination and exhaustive indexed list of all the material put before him, comprising almost all the deeds and papers up to about 1870 but only one or two volumes. He created the present system of Formal Archives. These were arranged in cabinets in the Bursary (at that time situated near the Library) and, reshaped only slightly by successive generations of Bursary Clerks, remain as the core of the College records.

In 1909 the well known Oxford and Essex antiquarian Andrew Clark (Balliol 1875) initiated a search for the Bursars' Books etc. which had been "dispersed into cellars and other obscure chambers", recording[9] that "no small difficulty was experienced in routing them out of their hiding places. The MSS had to be examined disorderly as they came to hand. It is certain that some have not yet been recovered." Oral tradition has it that about 1920 the books thus rescued were sent off for scrap but called back from destruction just in time, although not before being stripped of their boards in some cases. It was probably shortly after this experience that they were deposited in a cellar beneath the Junior Common Room, where they remained until about 1950, when they were listed and wrapped for the Library by E.G.W. Bill. The Library also acquired numerous other old volumes at various times, although the Senior or Estates Bursar remained nominally responsible for all Archives until the office of Archivist was established in 1981. The Bursary moved from the Library Passage across the Front Quadrangle to Staircase III in 1913, taking the Formal Archives with it. Unfortunately, Staircase III had a large damp cellar and much loose material of date ca. 1780 onwards was put in it: periodic additions of dead files were made up to 1965 when the Bursary moved again, leaving the contents to fester. The Formal Archives were again taken along but the cabinets did not fit into the new accommodation and they and their contents were distributed in stages between the Library and a most unsuitable small room nearby.

I was smitten with a dilettante interest in the College records about 1970 and started to take the matter seriously about 1975. At that time the bulk of the records in volumes was in the Library but was not catalogued, the Formal Archives were divided as explained already, and there was a vast amount of unexamined disordered material in the basement of Staircase III and the Bursary loft. A programme was undertaken with the aim of bringing archive material of all classes under the same ceiling, listing it, arranging it (as far as possible without disrupting previous partial arrangements) and restoring where necessary. Much remains to be done - the project is in any case open-ended - but some progress has been made. It is now possible to say with reasonable confidence that all the surviving pre-1939 records of the College have been identified and listed, and the entire collection (excepting a number of special items which remain in the Library) has been marshalled in a specially appointed Archive Room.

BALLIOL COLLEGE ARCHIVES

The description which follows in Section II draws heavily on previous work, especially that of George Parker. It has no pretensions to be a proper catalogue, and attempts only to give a general guide to the kind of material to be found and its extent. The present arrangement of the Archives (Section III) has evolved over a long period and is in many ways very illogical, and the description given is only loosely geared to it. The sub-section numbers used here thus do not lead directly to the actual material described: resort to the indexes and other aids mentioned in Section IV is necessary for that.

All College records except those less than thirty years old or which relate to living persons are normally available for consultation. Applications for access should be made in writing to the Archivist, who will also be glad to advise and deal with limited specific enquiries by correspondence.

"But the Author having had no natural Geny to the study of Antiquities and History ..... hath committed many foul Errors." Thus wrote Anthony Wood[10] of his friend Henry Savage, the first College Historian, three hundred years ago. I am glad to say that I have been luckier with my friends: I am grateful for their help and interest, especially the Master, Penny Bulloch, Vincent Quinn and the late Richard Hunt. Marilyn Howard laid out the text with great skill and was remarkably patient with my many revisions.

Balliol, 20 October 1983 John Jones

II THE COMPOSITION OF THE ARCHIVES

A. STATUTES, FOUNDATION DEEDS AND CHARTERS

Statutes, Statute Books, foundation deeds, copies and associated documents, 13th-20th centuries. The early Statutes etc. have mostly been printed by Salter[1] and translations are given by de Paravicini.[2] Facsimiles of the first Statutes and some early deeds are collected together in 'Domus de Balliolo'.[3]

The Statutes given by the Lady Dervorguilla, effective Foundress, 1282 (in excellent condition, with her seal intact), and related deeds, one of which mentions Richard Fitzralph in 1325.

The Statutes given by Sir Philip Somervyle, 1340.

An exemption from the payment of tenths, bearing an example of the Oxford Corporation seal, 1384.

Records (including a transcript of a Papal Bull of Urban V which was surrendered to the King in 1537) concerning a commission to revise the Statutes, 1363-1365, and further amendments of 1433, 1470 - but not the revised Statutes themselves, which were already lost by 1668.

Records (including a transcript of a Papal Bull of Julius II, also taken away by the King's agents in 1537) concerning a commission to revise the Statutes, 1504-1507.

Statute Books, 5 volumes:

(i). This contains a copy of the 1507 Statutes (n.d. but early 16th century) with later entries concerning amendments of 1571 and 1587, a Bell Exhibition agreement of 1558, and Visitors' decrees of 1789, 1802, 1834 and 1838.

(ii). This contains a copy of the 1507 Statutes made in 1627, with later entries which are similar to those in (i) but more numerous.

(iii). This contains a copy of the 1507 Statutes made in 1694, with later entries similar to those in (ii).

(iv). This contains a copy of the 1507 Statutes and principal later decrees, made in 1722, apparently as an exercise and or gesture of affection by Michael Ernle for his Tutor, William Best.

(v). This contains copies of the 1507 Statutes and principal later decrees, made in the 19th century.

A number of other Statute Books are known - there is one of the 17th century in the Library catalogued as MS 400 and others in the Library of St. Catherine's College Cambridge (L.III.18) and in the Bodleian Library (MS. Top.Oxon.e.160).

A Charter of Incorporation, 1588, inter alia confirming the College's style (previously variable) as 'The Master and Scholars of Balliol College'.

Minutes of special College Meetings concerning the revision of the Statutes, 1855-1857. 2 volumes.

Correspondence, drafts etc. concerning the Statutes and amendments to them, 19th century-1966. 2 boxes.

Copies of the Statutes as printed at various dates, 19th-20th centuries.

B. VISITORS

Records of the elections of Visitors (it is the College's unique privilege to elect its own Visitor), 17th-20th centuries, incomplete.

Decrees of and correspondence with Visitors concerning the Statutes and other matters, especially disputed elections, 13th-20th centuries. A list of Visitors since 1691 is given in Appendix A.

C. MEMBERSHIP

Until the early 16th century there is only fragmentary evidence for the membership of the College - principally names mentioned in deeds or in connection with the pledging of books. All likely sources have been sifted by Emden.[4]

1. Masters

A list of Masters is given in Appendix B.

(a) Elections

Elections are recorded in the Latin and English Registers. Some loose papers survive, most notably relating to the controversial election of Theophilus Leigh, 1726.

(b) Instruments of Admission

The series is practically complete from the admission of Thomas Cisson, 1511.

(c) Official correspondence

A modest amount survives, 17th-20th centuries, and more is to be found admixed with the private papers of recent Masters, 19th-20th centuries (see V.C).

2. Fellows

A list of Fellows since 1514 is available.

(a) Elections

Records of elections to Fellowships and College Offices are entered in the Latin and English Registers; access is most conveniently made via Clark's Annual Lists - see 3(a).

(b) Records of stipendiary and other payments

These survive from the 16th century.

3. Members in general

(a) Andrew Clark's Annual Lists

About 1900-1910, Clark examined the Registers and Bursars' Books and compiled a series of Annual Lists of members,1520-19th century, in ten volumes.

(i) 1520-1590, with explanatory notes

(ii)-(ix) 1591-1805

(x) 1806-1857, with a table of College Officers 1538-1868

Clark also compiled 'Tables illustrating the constitution of Balliol College 1520-1857' in two volumes, giving tables of succession in Fellowship and Exhibition places, numbers of members on the books, Fellowship dividends etc.

(b) Registers of admission, residence and degrees

The coverage from 1636 is exhaustive but somewhat confused by overlapping series.

(i) Admissions and degrees, 1636-1682. 1 volume. Two contemporary copies, one indexed, one with a table of fees.

(ii) Admissions and degrees,1682-1833. 1 volume. This volume also contains records of Oaths taken and corresponding Quarter Sessions certificates, 1715-1800. The official register of Chapel burials, 1819-1830, is inserted (three entries only - there have been no burials since 1830).

(iii) Admissions and degrees,1834-1893. 1 volume.

(iv) Admissions, 1870-1958. 3 volumes in which members entered their own names.

(v) College Officers' admissions records, 1858-1968. 10 volumes.

(vi) Admissions residence and degrees, 1892-1930. 1 volume.

(vii) Residence records, 1779-1895. 4 volumes, two of which also have degree records, 1832-1920.

(viii) Degrees, 1779-1837.

(ix) Birth and baptismal certificates presented by Scholars, and Fellows' instruments of resignation, ca. 1800-1850. 1 file.

(x) Room lists, 1857-1971, with gaps. 4 items.

(xi) Returns to the University of members on the College books, 1878-1968. 8 volumes.

(xii) Printed termly lists of members in residence, 1883-1969, lacking 1950-1952. 11 volumes.

(xiii) Continuations of (xii) but annual, 1970-1980.

The Admissions Registers usually give father's name, residence, and (less regularly) status: more information, including age and school, generally appears from about 1830. The records in (v) often supply detail not found elsewhere and also extend to unsuccessful candidates for admission. A few certificates and resignations earlier than those in (ix) are to be found inserted in the Latin Register.

(c) Individual Dossiers.

Dossiers containing papers regarding admission, and the academic (and often subsequent) careers of members deceased since about 1945. Correspondence of any individual with College Officers is likely to have been filed here. ca. 2000 files in one alphabetical sequence.

(d) Address Lists.

Printed Address Lists for living former members compiled in 1929, 1949, and 1962, with updating annotations to about 1970.

The College has published Registers[5] of its members 1833-1980 in which are given names, dates of birth, parentage, academic records, subsequent careers, marriages, publications and dates of death. Collected biographies have also been printed for members who fell in the Great War and Snell Exhibitioners 1699-1900.[6]

Courses for officer cadets were given in Balliol during both World Wars, but the records are very sparse:

'The Souvenir. A Coy.No.6. Officers Cadet Battalion Balliol College Oxford. November 10 1917-February 26, 1918.' Printed, with full lists of names (which are not recorded elsewhere), photographs etc.

Papers concerning the expenses of cadets, some of whom appear in the College Register, 1943-1945.

A number of German and Austrian refugee scholars were taken in by the College 1938-9. A little about some of them can be discovered from the minutes of College Meetings, but records are otherwise lacking.

D. GOVERNMENT

1. College Meetings

(a) Latin Registers

3 volumes,1514-1916.

(i) 1514-1682. This Register, which is almost entirely in Latin, records admissions of Masters, elections, appointments, leave of absence, admonitions, expulsions, presentations, etc. Visitors' decrees and other documents which were considered to be of particular importance are often copied in or inserted. Some estates and financial matters are noted, e.g. details of losses in the Great Fire of London, lease memoranda, fees and charges, a list of plate sold 1668. Allocations of rooms in College to Fellows begin to be entered from about

1600. There are occasional records of deaths and burial in the Chapel. Other items of particular interest include memoranda of Chapel building contracts (ca. 1520) and a list made in 1568 of 152 pre-reformation Benefactors (see Emden[7]). The first 80 pages, which have rather scrappy entries 1514-1570,are largely transcribed or translated by de Paravicini[2] who also gives a number of later sections.

(ii) 1682-1781. The content of this Register is much the same as its predecessor, but it is for the most part better kept and more detail appears. From about 1730 inserted nominations, certificates etc. regarding appointments to the Snell, Warner and other foundations are numerous.

(iii) 1782-1916. This Register continues from (ii) but is much more restricted in content after 1794 when the English Register (see below) becomes the main record of corporate acts except for elections, disciplinary matters and so on - but even these soon begin to appear in the English Register and the Latin Register is scrappy from about 1840, finally petering out in 1916.

(b) English Registers

14 volumes of minutes, 1794-1976, covering all manner of administrative, financial, estates and academic business in considerable detail. A transcript of the first volume (1794-1875) is available. Fully indexed from about 1925.

(c) Rough minutes

The minutes in (b) above are as composed after the meetings. For two periods there are also the on the spot notes of the Master or Keeper of the Minutes. 5 volumes, 1805-1809 and 1893-1918.

2. Committees

Loose 20th century committee working papers survive in abundance, but are not complete and are rather scattered. Some of the following are in proper Minute Books, but most are gatherings of papers.

(a) Executive Committee minutes
1968-1977

(b) Tutorial Board minutes
1963-1979

(c) Academic Committee minutes
1963-1966

(d) Financial Committee minutes
1933-1956 and 1964-1969

(e) Buildings Committee minutes
1959-1978

(f) Estates Committee minutes
1966-1978

E. BENEFACTIONS

The College's major Benefactors are named in Appendix C. A complete list of Benefactors 1263-1864, with notes on their gifts, was compiled by Henry Wall in 1865.

1. Loose Records

Legal documents, trust deeds, correspondence with Benefactors and their executors, sometimes with copies of relevant wills, 13th-20th centuries. There are numerous files concerning bequests and gifts, many of which concern special Fellowships etc. (for a list of names see Appendix D).

2. Benefaction Books

4 volumes,1636-1783.

3. Appeal Records

Correspondence, accounts and papers concerning Appeals and resulting Funds, especially the Endowment Fund (1904), the War Memorial Fund (1919), and the Septcentenary Appeal (1963).

F. PLATE

A survey of the College Silver is given by Willis-Bund.[8]

1. Inventories and valuations

ca. 30 items,1598-20th century.

2. Catalogue

A catalogue compiled by D.W. Jackson, completed in 1981. In five volumes: an exhaustive photographic survey with commentary giving weights, dates, history and points of interest.

G. SPECIAL FELLOWSHIPS, SCHOLARSHIPS, EXHIBITIONS AND PRIZES

See also E. above. Records connected with a large number of foundations come under this heading. The most prominent concern the Blundell Fellowships and Scholarships (17th-20th centuries), the Jowett Lectureships and Fellowships (19th-20th centuries) and the Snell and Warner Exhibitions (17th-20th centuries). For a fuller list see Appendix D.

1. Loose Records

Correspondence, trust deeds, copies of relevant wills, and litigation papers concerning the orginal endowments and variations in terms and conditions. 17th-20th centuries.

2. Accounts and other Records of Trust Funds

These often give details of recipients which are not found in other sources. Mostly 17th-19th centuries.

3. Certificates, Nominations, and Resignations

The Latin Register has several examples from the 18th century, especially for the Snell and Warner Foundations. There is also a separate file for the same, 1800-1850.

H. ESTATES AND ECCLESIASTICAL PATRONAGE

1. Estates

The College no longer holds much agricultural or urban property, and all its ancient estates have been disposed of. Material relating to all the estates the College has ever administered is surveyed here, without differentiation between those vested in the College itself (i.e. Domus estates), those managed for College trusts, and those connected with College livings. Domus, trust and patronage business is in any case frequently found to be inextricably intertwined.

(a) Loose records

The loose estates records are mostly organised by county and property. They comprise documentation relating to title, leases etc. from mediaeval times; surveys, reports on visits for inspection, lists of tenants, terriers, maps and plans, valuations, litigation papers, insurance papers, correspondence, accounts, sale particulars etc. increase in volume from the sixteenth to the present century. There are a few Manor Court items. The records often cover a much longer span than the College's ownership - the Buttermere estate, for example, was only in the College's hands for a few years in modern times but documents since the sixteenth century were acquired when the estate was bought and retained when it was sold. The material is very voluminous from about 1820, falling off between 1920 and 1960 as the principal estates were sold off. Because several of the estates were very distant, agents were employed: their reports and accounts are of particular interest. The principal properties are listed below.

Bedfordshire

Beeston in the parish of Sandy

A small farm and lands, including Balliol College Meadow

ca. 15 items,1615-1799.

Buckinghamshire

Great Linford

1 item, a single leaf 'A Note of the Gleab And Chripses Land', 1658 - a detailed survey of lands at least partly in Great Linford, with field names and areas.

Marlow

1 item, a single leaf 'Seymour's Court Survey by The Rump 1649' - a survey of lands at least partly in Marlow, with field names, areas and valuations.

Hambledon and Medmenham

Burrow Farm and Woods

ca. 100 items,1250-1898 and a file 1883-1892.

Princes Risborough

A farm in the hamlet of Loosely Row, including the moieties North's and Saunder's

ca. 25 items,1622-1885.

Cumberland

Buttermere Estate in the parishes of Brackenthwaite, Buttermere, Lorton and Loweswater. Including Lanthwaite Green Farm, Low Hollins

Farm, High Hollins Farm, Oakbank Farm, Netherclose Farm, Rannerdale Farm, Croft House Farm, Wilkinsyke Farm, Pottergill, Bowderbeck Cottage and Bowderbeck Barn.

ca. 160 items,1581-1959 and 10 files 1934-1963.

Devon

Braunton

A small estate known as Lobb Philip

ca. 10 items,1792-1881 and 2 files 1889-1896.

Stoodleigh

Thorn's Farm

ca. 25 items,1654-1921 and a file 1884-1891.

Gloucestershire

Tirley and Chaceley

Little Cumberwood Farm, partly in Tirley and partly in Chaceley

ca. 60 items,1391-1893.

Huntingdonshire

Abbotsley

Lands associated with the Rectory

ca. 200 items,1256-1951.

London

Clerkenwell

A number of houses and gardens near St. James' Church in St. James' Walk

ca. 100 items,1490-1920.

St. Lawrence Jewry

The parsonage house etc.

ca. 150 items 1180-1950. John Wycliffe is mentioned in 1360. Some of the early deeds are discussed by Barron.[9] The earliest in the series, a grant of the Abbot of Montreuil of about 1180, is also the oldest document in the entire collection: it is reproduced in 'Domus de Balliolo'.[3]

St. Margaret Pattens

Tenements at the corner of Rood Lane and East Cheap 1376-1837

ca. 50 items and two files,1911-1927. George Neville is mentioned in 1462.

Various other properties in London and Greater London

ca. 20 items and 10 files,19th-20th centuries.

Northamptonshire

Culworth

Happylands farm

2 files,1938-1953.

Greatworth

The Malt House etc.

4 files,1947-1951.

Marston St. Lawrence

An estate including Manor Farm, Washpool Farm, Kytle Farm, Westhorp Farm, Marston Hill Farm, Costow Farm, Blencowe's Farm

ca. 30 files,1919-1971.

Sulgrave

Stuchbury Manor Farm

2 files,1942-1960

Northumberland

Long Benton (alias Mickle or Great Benton) and Stamfordham

Farms at Long Benton, Stamfordham and The Heugh in Stamfordham, including Long Benton Farm, Scotts House Farm, Westerheugh Farm,

Upper Heugh Farm, Hawkwell House etc.

ca. 600 items,1323-1974,and 20 files,19th-20th centuries.

Oxfordshire

Headington

A quarry

1 item, 1613.

Moreton near Thame

A farm

ca. 80 items,1286-1863. George Neville is mentioned in 1464, 1475.

Nethercote, Tackley

A small estate

ca. 25 items,1563-1850.

Northmoor

ca. 50 items,1150-1428.

Oddington

A small estate

ca. 40 items,1300-1869.

Oxford City

Various properties

ca. 800 items,13th-20th centuries, and 50 files,19th-20th centuries. Almost all the pre-1850 documents are printed in full or summarised by Salter.[1]

Steeple Aston

Balliol Meadow, near the course of the railway close to Lower Heyford station

ca. 50 items,1200-1858. The earliest document in this group in fact concerns Kennington: its only obvious link with the others is that it has been kept with them for at least three centuries. One of the deeds of 1321 has been printed and discussed by Fryde and Highfield:[10] it recites the whole membership of the College, mentioning Thomas Bradwardine.

Woodstock and Wootton

Various farms and other properties including 'The George' alias 'The Marlborough Arms', Praunces Place, Manor Farm, Parrotts, College Farm etc.

ca. 400 items, 13th-19th centuries, and 10 files, 19th-20th centuries. George Neville is mentioned in 1462, 1465; Cuthbert Tunstall in 1517, 1541, and 1549; there is a detailed plan and elevation of 'The George', 1794.

Radnor

Llanbister

Lands at Davendour

3 items, 18th century.

Llandeilo Graban

An estate including Llandeilo Hall

ca. 40 items, 1657-1873.

Scotland

Easter Balblair

As far as is known the College has never had any estates in Scotland, but there is in the Archives a very lengthy detailed draft setting out the disposition of Easter Balblair (near Cromarty) lands, ferry, alehouses etc, by George Dallas, 1695. No link is obvious, but the document may be a stray from the Library Strachan Davidson Papers, which include material relating to estates in Scotland (mostly at Ardgraith in the parish of Errol, near Perth, however).

Shropshire

Culmington and Siefton

2 items, 18th century.

Somerset

Cutcombe and Timberscombe

Farms and other properties including Guns, Well, West Stowey, Capersland and Hammett's Cleeve

ca. 10 items, 1701-1896.

Warwickshire

Ufton

An estate taking in almost all the village, including 'The White Hart' Inn, Tithe Farm, Hill Farm, Posher Farm, Island Farm, Home Farm, Wood Farm, Town Farm, Colborne Farm etc.

ca. 750 items, 17th-20th centuries, and 25 files, 19th-20th centuries.

Worcestershire

Suckley

Farms and other properties including Bennett's, Plaister's, Havingtree Farm, and Lower House Farm

ca. 35 items, 17th-19th centuries.

(b) Books

Lease Books

Registers of leases granted and other legal instruments executed by the College.

7 volumes, 1588-1950.

Lease Log-book or Fine Book

A log of leases granted, with comments on the circumstances, arranged by property. The Oxford entries are printed by Salter.[1]

1 volume, 1588-1850.

Rent Books

The Bursars' Half-yearly and Annual Accounts are practically the sole source of rent data up to the late 19th century, but there are Rent Rolls giving great detail in 8 volumes, 1886-1960.

Survey Book

Most surveys are with the loose records,but there is a substantial one in book form: 'Particulars of Huntspill Rectory Manor & Freehold Estate Somersetshire', 1870. Details of occupants are given, as well as precise particulars and valuations.

(c) Maps

The loose estates records contain a large number of maps and plans. The substantial and significant ones of date 1850 and earlier are as follows:

Buckinghamshire

Hambleden and Medmenham

A series of maps of Burrow Farm Estate, based on surveys made by Richard Comley (1616), John Ricler (1701), Richard Davis (1795) and William Rutt (1806).

Cumberland

Buttermere.

'A Plan of an Estate situated at Buttermere the property of John Marshall Esq' by Jonathan Stanmix (1838).

Devon

Stoodleigh

'A plan of an Estate called Thorn's lying in the Parish of Stoodley in the County of Devon belonging to Baliol College Oxford' by Robert Leave (1770).

Gloucestershire

Tirley and Chaceley

A survey of an Estate in the Parishes of Tirley and Chaceley, by Richard Davis (ca. 1780),and a map of Little Cumberwood Estate, by W. Price (1850).

Northumberland

Long Benton and Stamfordham

A series of maps by William Donkin and William Weleands (1767), J. Fryer (1801, 1802) and Richard Jenkyns, Master of the College (ca. 1820).

Oxfordshire

Steeple Aston

A plan of lands let at Steeple Aston, by R. Davis (1793).

Wootton

A plan of lands in the parish of Wootton by Lewis Andrewes (1687); and another by William Rutt (1805); a 'Plan of Mr. Thomas Sotham's Estate, Wootton', printed by C.M. Firth, n.d. but 1837.

Radnorshire

Llanbister

A plan of 1757.

Shropshire

Culmington and Siefton

Plans by Thomas Sherrif (1757, 1760).

Somerset

Timsbury

A plan of 1784.

Warwickshire

Ufton

'A Plot of the Lordship of Ufton' by Thomas Hewitt (1695).

2. Ecclesiastical Patronage

The College's current ecclesiastical patronage is summarised annually in the Oxford University Calendar.

(a) Loose records

The loose ecclesiastical patronage records are mostly arranged by living. They comprise documents relating to title and to presentations (often dating from well before the acquisition of the advowson), and correspondence and miscellaneous papers (sparse before 1700, becoming more extensive to 1880 and voluminous thereafter). The correspondence and miscellaneous papers are very varied, including letters from and about prospective incumbents, valuations and surveys, correspondence about repairs to church and parsonage fabric, correspondence with Bishops about proposed appointments and unions with other livings etc. A few of the files contain maps: several contain some printed material (postcards, church guides, parish magazines etc). The principal livings (some of which have been held with shifting combinations of others not mentioned) are listed below:

Abbotsley

Advowson acquired 1341

ca. 70 items,1256-1951,and 4 files,1883-1946. John Wycliffe is mentioned several times ca. 1360.

Aston Flamville with Burbage

Advowson acquired 1919

1 file,1916-1940.

Bedford, St. Mary's

Advowson acquired 1855

2 files,1894-1902 and 1925-1945.

Bere Regis

Advowson acquired 1699

ca. 10 items,1558-1868,and 4 files,1899-1939.

Blunham

Advowson acquired 1919

5 files,1918-1948.

Brattleby

Advowson acquired 1343, sold 1878

ca. 10 items,1342-1837,and 1 file.

Calstone

Advowson acquired 1692, subsequently alienated

No loose documents after 1701.

Clophill

Advowson acquired 1919

3 files,1919-1954.

Colchester

The advowsons of several Colchester livings were acquired in 1714: there have been numerous complicated changes and additions resulting from reorganisation, exchanges and gifts. See Clark.[11]

ca. 50 items,1537-1927,and 11 files,1893-1947.

Duloe

Advowson acquired 1705

ca.70 items,1562-1860,and 4 files,1887-1946.

Fillingham

Advowson acquired 1343

ca. 15 items,1342-1852,and 2 files,1891-1897 and 1913-1954.

Fordham

Advowson acquired 1921

1 file,1921-1936.

Great Horkesley

Advowson acquired 1921

1 file,1927-1941.

Harrold

Advowson acquired 1919

1 item,1925, and 1 file,1917-1952.

Huntspill

Advowson acquired 1724

ca. 100 items,1701-1938,and 3 files,1896-1966.

Kilve

Advowson acquired 1688, sold 1892.

ca. 10 items,1688-1873,and 1 file,1887-1891.

Leire

Advowson acquired 1919

1 file,1921-1943.

London St. Lawrence Jewry

Advowson acquired 1294, reluctantly surrendered 1951.

ca. 100 items,1180-1947, and 4 files,1894-1951.

Long Benton

Advowson acquired 1340

ca. 100 items,1323-1969, and 2 files,1912-1946.

Marks Tey

Advowson acquired 1722, sold 1877

No loose documents.

Pulloxhill with Flitton

Advowson acquired 1919

1 file,1927-1954.

Riseholme

Advowson acquired 1343, exchanged 1855

ca. 15 items,1342-1949.

South Luffenham

Advowson acquired 1855

ca. 40 items,1694-1881, and 1 file,1930-1949. See also the Kilve file,1887-1891.

Tendring

Advowson acquired 1714

ca. 15 items,1615-1865, and 1 file,1903-1946. See also Colchester items and files.

Timsbury

Advowson acquired 1701

ca. 50 items,1634-1873, and 2 files,1896-1952.

Ulceby cum Fordington

Advowson acquired 1942

ca. 40 items,1702-1937, and 1 file,1941-1965.

Estates and patronage business intermingles at all periods and loose material concerning patronage is also to be found with estates papers.

There is a General and Miscellaneous file of patronage papers 1890-1952 which includes the following items of special interest:

A draft (6 pp) 'Memorandum as to the approximate market value of the Advowsons of Sundry Livings of which the Master and Scholars of Balliol College Oxford are the Patrons', Jan. 1890 (Duloe, Fillingham, Kilve with Stringston, South Luffenham).

A detailed report (4 pp) on a visit to the College livings in Bedfordshire (Harrold, Clophill, Flitton and Pulloxhill), 24-25 Mar 1920, by the Master.

(b) Books

There are no Patronage Books as such, but the College Latin and English Registers contain information about patronage business, with especially useful detail from the beginning of the first English Register (1794) until about 1950. The Lease Books contain not only leases but also copies of other deeds executed by the College, including presentations to livings. See also the Bursars' Book concerning the Williams Benefaction for the benefit and purchase of College livings.

I. BUILDINGS

For a concise account of the College architecture see Sherwood and Pevsner.[12]

BALLIOL COLLEGE ARCHIVES

1. Plans of the College

An original 'Ichnographia' of 1695, which has been published,[13] survives: the other sources for the pre-19th century layout of the College are all printed (see Salter[1]). The Bodleian Library has a plan of 1848.[14] The College has especially detailed large scale plans of 1882 and 1949.

2. Architects' Designs

There are numerous plans, drawings and designs - including some never executed - notably by the following:

James Wyatt, 1790.

George Basevi, 1825-1843. Residential buildings etc.

A.W.N. Pugin, 1843. Controversial proposals: see Bryson.[15]

Alfred and Paul Waterhouse, 1867-1910. Hall, residential buildings.

E.P. Warren, 1905-1925. Residential buildings.

T.G. Jackson, 1911. Chapel.

More recent architectural drawings are very numerous indeed: the principal architects engaged on the College itself since 1950 have been Sir Edward Maufe and G.J. Beard.

3. Building Contracts, Accounts and Correspondence with Architects

There are contracts, accounts and correspondence connected with the drawings and building operations mentioned in 2. above. Additionally there are the following:

A deed mentioning gifts by Nicholas de Quappelade, Abbot of Reading, for the building of a Chapel, 1328.

Memoranda of agreements with John Lobbens, William Jonsons and William Eist regarding the building of a Chapel, 1522-1528.

Accounts, and Henry Keene's receipts, regarding the building of a residential block, the Fisher Building, 1768-1771.

Anthony Salvin's receipt and John Kelk's estimate regarding the building of a residential block, 1853.

Correspondence with William Butterfield, architect of the Chapel, 1854-1860, and miscellaneous related papers.

Correspondence and papers concerning the reconstruction of the Master's Lodgings, 1948-1950.

Further details are to be found in the Bursars' Books, and in the Registers.

J. DOMESTIC ADMINISTRATION AND FINANCIAL AFFAIRS

1. Half-yearly Bursars' Accounts (Computi)

13 volumes 1568-1844, in good condition with very few gaps and imperfections. An earlier volume 1544-1568 was seen and largely transcribed by Clark[16] about 1910 but is now missing. Summaries of regular income and expenditure of all kinds are given, with details of miscellaneous expenditure - 'Minutae Expensae', later 'Contingents'. Latin, of a cryptic and inventive kind, is generally used except for 1575-1637 and 1816-1844. A typical list of early seventeenth century Minutae Expensae might contain 50-60 detailed entries covering minor building works, kitchen equipment, gardens, fuel, charitable donations, hospitality, pump maintenance, legal expenses, cleaning, clearing the privies, carriage of supplies, chains for the library, estates repairs, expenditure on feasts etc. The pattern continues but gradually falls into a briefer and stereotyped style, with much less detail after about 1750 until the early 19th century, when there is an expansion and academic expenses begin to appear. The general character of the entries seems to be similar to those in the Lincoln College Accounts which are quoted by Green.[17]

2. Annual Bursars' Accounts

11 volumes, 1672-1883; printed annual accounts, 1865-1981; mostly in excellent order. These accounts are more formal than the half yearly accounts but nevertheless often have detail which complements the latter up to 1844. From 1845 the practice of drawing up half yearly accounts was abandoned and the last three volumes of handwritten accounts 1845-1883 are very detailed.

3. Battels and Buttery Books

'Battels' is Oxford jargon for an individual's College bill. Some 600 volumes and parcels, 1576-20th century with few gaps, but many volumes are in a mutilated and/or fragile state. The chief interest of these is in connection with membership and residence: Clark digested them for his Annual Lists (see II.C.3).

4. Caution Money Books

'Caution Money' is the payment still made, albeit at token level, by new members to guarantee their credit.

7 volumes, 1610-1926.

5. Bursars' Ledgers and Miscellaneous Books

Some 500 volumes, 16th-20th centuries, although the majority are of the 19th-20th centuries. Of particular interest are the following:

Ledgers

1670-1671, 1671-1672. These have greater detail than the other accounts of the period.

Treasury Books

1637-1689 and 1689-1712, 1829-1855. These record movements of deeds and cash in and out of the Treasury.

Arrears Books

17th-19th centuries. Accounts and notes regarding members in arrears with battels payments. 6 volumes.

Rent and Miscellaneous Book

1 volume, most entries ca. 1655; a rough notebook of details of bursarial transactions; includes a long table of wheat and malt prices at frequent intervals, 1615-1689.

Weekly Battels Books

5 volumes, 1922-1958. These are in excellent order and complete. They provide easy access to the battels of individuals in this period.

Books concerning Scholarships etc.

13 volumes, 1868-1971; accounts and other records regarding payments to Scholars, Exhibitioners etc.

Senior Common Room Books

Charges to Fellows on battels, 1871-1879, 1929-1935 and 1939-1960 which reveal details of their residence and social activity.

Subscription Books

18 volumes, 1892-1973, recording subscriptions to Societies etc. made by individuals via battels. These enable the nature and extent of an individual's participation in College life to be discovered.

6. Room Lists

19th-20th centuries, but with many gaps.

7. Tradesmens' Accounts and Receipts

18th-20th centuries, but relatively few in number. A fairly full group of the late 18th century is of interest giving, e.g. details of gardening and building work done, Common Room expenditure etc. In the 16th-17th centuries tradesmens' receipts are often written directly into the Bursars' half-yearly account books.

8. Inventories

17th-20th centuries, including complete inventories of furniture: 1640 (the entire College); 1934 (F.F. Urquhart's rooms); 1939 (Staircases I-XVI); and 1949 (the Master's Lodgings).

9. Domestic Staff

The names of College employees can often be found in the Bursars' account books from the 16th century. More systematic sources - wages books, pension records etc. - exist from about 1870 to the present day,but are incomplete.

Written instructions regarding the duties of porters, staircase servants etc. survive from the early 19th century.

10. Printed Ephemera

Rules and Regulations, notices, circulars etc, 19th-20th centuries. This class includes material solicited from most of the other Colleges for comparative purposes at times when the College was reviewing its own rules and charges - there are especially full collections for 1912, 1948 and 1964.

11. Bonds

About 100 loose bonds given to or by the College, mostly 1550-1750, including bonds given on appointment by manciples etc. and bonds given by tradesmen with whom the College deposited modest sums (e.g. £100 with Henry Clements the bookseller in 1710, interest at 5% still being paid by Daniel Prince in 1770). Bonds (e.g. guaranteeing payment of battels) are sometimes found written directly into the early Bursars' Books.

12. Investment and Banking Records

18th-20th centuries, including records relating to the College in account with Childs Bank, 1781-1885.

13. Gardens

The Bursars' Books contain occasional entries for expenditure on the gardens at all periods. There are also some loose papers, notably the following:

Bills, with great detail, from Robert Penson and James Tagg, for ornamental trees and shrubs supplied for a replanting programme, 1793-1794.

A botanically exact list of trees, shrubs and wall plants planted, 1904-1926.

A botanically exact list of shrubs and trees around the walls, 1980.

14. Correspondence

19th-20th centuries, very substantial in amount. The Bursars' Letter Books of 1888-1919 (20 volumes) are of particular interest because of their completeness.

K. DEPARTMENTS

1. The Balliol Trinity Laboratories

These Laboratories flourished 1853-1939, and were towards the end of their life effectively the University Department of Physical Chemistry: see Smith.[16] Accounts, fee books and attendance records survive, with some loose papers and photographs.

2. Chapel

Licences survive permitting the College to have its own Oratory, and subsequently Chapel, 1293-1364. Records relating to Chapel building works have been covered under II.I. The 16th and 17th century Bursars' Books have regular entries for Chapel running expenses and minor works. Such expenses appear in Deans' Books later: these have been preserved for 1740-1810 and 1841-1881. There is a considerable amount of Bursars' correspondence concerning fittings and furniture 19th-20th centuries. A few 20th century printed forms of service, termly programmes etc. have been kept.

3. Holywell Manor

Holywell Manor House, parts of which are of ancient construction, has been a College Annexe since 1930. Balliol has no material relating to it earlier than this. A brief history was written by Galbraith in 1937.[19] A further block was built nearby in 1966: the whole complex now serves graduates only. The records comprise the following:

Acquisition papers, correspondence etc., dealing with the lease-purchase from Merton College, 1929.

Fund-raising papers. Mostly 1928-1932, including a Register of Contributors.

Papers regarding 1930 building works and early days, 1930-1940. With some plans. Papers concerning the murals by Gilbert Spencer and the associated controversy; the layout of the gardens; the opening ceremony; initial administration.

Records of building works,1966. Correspondence with Sir Leslie Martin, architect, accounts and other papers.

Accounts. 6 volumes,1928-1949.

Administrative papers. 1940-1980, including a full inventory of 1955, files relating to the establishment of Holywell Manor as a Balliol - St. Anne's College Graduate Institution 1960-1970, a file to do with the restoration of the Gilbert Spencer murals in 1979, etc.

L. STUDENT LIFE

1. Studies

There is little to be found about undergraduate studies anywhere in College records before about 1775, because the arrangements between a Tutor and his pupils were previously a matter of private contract. Payments for tuition and other academic expenses begin to appear in the Bursars' Books during the last quarter of the 18th century. The English Registers, and to a lesser extent the Latin Register, chronicle academic matters from about 1810: in recent years the minutes of Tutorial Board and the Academic Committee (see II.D.2) are the main source. There are two other classes of particular interest:

(a) Records of Collections

It has been the custom in Balliol since about 1805 for members to have their work assessed by their Tutors in the presence of the Master at the end of each term - 'Collections', 'Examinations' or 'Handshaking'. Records of these occasions are extant for 1812-1825, 1833-1841, 1841-1846, 1846-1852, 1852-1868, 1872-1873 and for men matriculating 1922-1925. Up to 1868 there is considerable detail, extending to lists of prescribed books and Tutors' comments.

(b) Tuition accounts

19th-20th centuries, incomplete. These record payments for teaching done and are of value for the identification of Tutors who were not Fellows, which sometimes presents problems.

2. Discipline

The Latin and English Registers of all periods mention disciplinary matters but rarely with much detail. Practically no other records of individual offences have been preserved but there is a Deans' Book, 1936-1951, with notes on disciplinary conventions, penalties etc. Many editions of the printed Rules, 19th-20th centuries, are available and there is substantial material relating to the topic of discipline in general, 1965-1975.

In 1850, Henry Wall (Fellow 1839-1871), who was of a litigious disposition, protested to the Visitor over, inter alia, the way disciplinary matters had been taken over by the Master and Tutors, contrary to the letter of the Statutes. His lengthy submission (which was accompanied by extensive extracts of disciplinary resolutions from the Latin Registers ca. 1750-1850) and the counter-arguments of the Master

(Richard Jenkyns) and his colleagues E.C. Woollcombe, W.C. Lake and Benjamin Jowett are full of information about attitudes on the subject.

3. Sport

Athletics records
1913-1933.

Boat Club records
Journals, accounts, and printed ephemera, 1835-1966.

Gordouli Boat Club minutes
1927-1971. This is a club for the sporting élite, not only oarsmen.

Cricket Club records
1900-1928, 1952-1954.

Hockey Club records
1902-1934.

Soccer Club records
1899-1929.

The Soviet minutes
1928-1932. This was a society 'constituted to propagate the principles of communism through the medium of Association Football'.

Tennis Club records
1904-1929.

United Athletic Clubs (later Amalgamated Clubs)
Accounts, minutes and miscellaneous papers, 1880-1976.

4. Societies

(a) Literary, Debating and Dining Societies

Programmes, minutes and printed ephemera survive for the following societies:

Arnold Society
1897-1967.

Brackenbury Society
1890-1914, with gaps.

Arnold and Brackenbury Society
1955-1968.

Dervorguilla Society
1930-1939.

Gibbon Club
1928-1941.

Hanover Club
1911-1913.

History Club
1907-1909.

Leonardo Society
1921-1939, 1945-1962.

Synoptic Club
1930-1935.

Younger Society
1927-1933, 1946-1956.

There is also some miscellaneous material relating to societies and their activities, including the Dining Book of an unidentified society, 1900-1910.

(b) Musical Society

Collected concert programmes, minutes and accounts,1885-1981.

(c) Dramatic Societies

A notebook of the Shakespeare Society, 1867-8, gives the names of members, plays read and cast lists, and there is a box of miscellaneous material relating to the Balliol Players, 1923-1978.

5. Junior Common Room

General Meeting Minutes
1903-1932, 1944-1952, 1959-1965, 1966-1975, 1978-1981.

Committee Meeting Minutes
1903-1932, 1944-1952, 1958-1965, 1967-1975.

Accounts
1890-1950.

Betting Books
1945-1946, 1948-1951 and 1965.

Suggestions Books
ca. 100 volumes,1919-1972.

Lists of Officers
1948-1980.

Miscellaneous papers, mostly post-1960, on a wide range of subjects, including the new Junior Common Room and its opening by H.M. King Olav of Norway in 1964, refugee students etc.

M. PHOTOGRAPHS

1. Occasions

Recording visits by Heads of State or Government, 19th-20th centuries.

2. Buildings

Photographs of buildings are numerous, but the collection is not as good as the one in the Oxford City Central Library. 19th-20th centuries. Of particular interest are those which show features now destroyed or concealed:

The Old Hall, interior, about 1865.

The Library during conversion work in 1959, showing the arches of the mediaeval screens passage.

Chapel interiors, about 1880.

The College from Broad Street, about 1860.

Views in the Garden Quadrangle before and during rebuilding works, 1960-1965.

A house in St. Giles next to the back gate, about 1906.

Views of old buildings just inside the back gate, shortly before demolition, about 1960.

The Balliol-Trinity Laboratories, 20th century.

3. Groups

Posed groups, often but not invariably with identifications, both mounted for framing and in albums. Very numerous indeed, including the following:

Matriculation Groups, 1914, 1935, 1949-1981.

Members of the Junior Common Room, 1879, 1888, 1891-1911, 1922-1925, 1926-1935, 1942-1960.

Members of the Senior Common Room, 1867-1869, 1912, 1940, 1945.

Boat Club, 1860-1959. 17 large albums.

Other Sports, 1884-1938. 5 large albums.

4. Societies

Arnold Society,1898.

Arnold and Brackenbury Society,1956.

Brackenbury Society,1870-1910.

Dervorguilla Society,1873-1909, 1925, 1930.

Younger Society,1948, 1955, 1957.

N. GENERAL MISCELLANY

1. Portraits

The principal College portraits are described in Mrs. R.L. Poole's catalogue, published 1925.[20] The Bursars' Books and English Registers contain occasional references to the painting of portraits and there are a number of files of loose papers, including:

Correspondence about Archbishop A.C. Tait's portrait (including autograph letters by Robert Browning and Matthew Arnold, 1885), 1884-1929.

Correspondence with H.R. Hope-Pinker about Benjamin Jowett's bust, 1894.

Papers concerning A.L. Smith's portrait by F. Dodd, 1914-1915.

Papers concerning Viscount Grey's portrait by James Guthrie, 1928.

2. Coins

Papers concerning J.L. Strachan Davidson's collection of ancient coins, 1880-1954.

3. Seal Matrices

The matrix of the 'First Seal', said to be 13th century. Its first known use was in 1341: its last in 1575. See Salter.[1]

The matrix of the 'Second Seal', said to be 15th century. No example of its use has so far been identified. See Salter.[1]

Two similar matrices of the seal in use since about 1580.

The First Seal is a large pointed oval which shows the Virgin and Child above Collegiate buildings supported by John Balliol and Dervorguilla his wife. The Second Seal is also a pointed oval but is much smaller, showing St. Catherine standing crowned holding a small wheel and sword beneath a canopy. The seal which came into use about 1580 is a large rounded oval showing a buxom crowned St. Catherine with no canopy, holding a large wheel and sword.

4. Blundell's School

A.D. Lindsay's papers as a Governor of Blundell's School, 1917-1934.

5. New Inn Hall

Balliol purchased the site of New Inn Hall in 1878 and subsequently absorbed its assets and members. The site was sold in 1895. There are papers concerning the purchase and sale (with some detailed plans) and the members of New Inn Hall affected by the takeover. New Inn Hall records which passed to Balliol include about 20 volumes of Battels Books, Buttery Books, Accounts etc. of the period 1830-1887 and an Admissions Register for 1831-1886.

6. J.W. Nicholson

Material concerning the affairs and lunacy of J.W. Nicholson FRS[21], 1921-1940.

7. T.S. Eliot

Correspondence between A.D. Lindsay and T.S. Eliot and other papers concerning N.M. Iovetz-Tereshchenko and his book 'Friendship-Love', 1938-1947. Eliot's letters, about a dozen in number (one of them in his own hand), are of 1941-1943.[22]

8. Robert Browning

Correspondence about the manuscript of 'Asolando', mostly 1912-1913.

9. College Stamps

Balliol, following the lead of other colleges, had its own stamps printed for use in the inter-college messenger service in 1885, but they were never issued because there was a clamp-down on this breach of the Post Office monopoly in 1886.[23] Numerous specimens have appeared on the philately market: there are several examples in the Archives, mostly in strips with tête-bêche pairs in the centre.

10. Eastman House

Papers, accounts, correspondence, inventories etc. concerning the official residence of the George Eastman Visiting Professors (for a list see the fifth edition of the College Register), 1930-1976.

11. Vice-Chancellor's Accounts

Roger Mander's accounts as Vice-Chancellor, 1700-1702.

12. Benjamin Jowett's Visitors' Book

The Master's Lodgings Visitors' Book for 1882-1893, the last decade of Benjamin Jowett's Mastership. Guests generally signed against the date; many a famous signature appears (Robert Browning several times).

13. The Balliol Boys' Club

A Boys' Club in South Oxford was started with Balliol support in 1907 and consolidated in 1921 as a memorial to Keith Rae (Balliol 1907). It flourished until the late sixties, when it was swallowed by City developments.[24] The 1921 endowment survives as the Keith Rae Trust which supports youth clubs and similar organisations. Material about the Club in the Archives is sparse but includes:

The Declaration of Trust, 1921.

'The Opening of Keith Rae House Oxford. Saturday November 19th, 1921', printed, 1921. A brief history of the Club to 1921, and an account of its activities etc, including detailed plans of the house.

A brass plaque commemorating Keith Rae (killed in France, 1915).

The Club War Memorial for 1914-1918, listing 39 names.

14. The Workers' Educational Association

Balliol was closely connected with the Workers' Educational Association (W.E.A.) and related movements as a result of the activities of A.L. Smith (Fellow 1882-1916, Master 1916-1924) and A.D. Lindsay (Fellow 1906-1922, Master 1924-1949) through whose offices it was also regularly the venue for W.E.A. Summer Schools.[25] Two files are of particular interest:

A.D. Lindsay's papers,mostly of ca. 1909,concerning the W.E.A. (including a few letters of William Temple) together with Wilson Wilson Fund papers,1929-1959. George Wilson Wilson (died 1925) made a bequest to the College to be used for the promotion of working-class education.

Correspondence with William Miles (1883-1972), drafts, newspaper cuttings etc. connected with, inter alia, his autobiography 'William Miles. An Autobiography' (1972), 1971-1972. He was actively involved in W.E.A. committees from 1907, and attended Balliol Summer Schools regularly 1913-1930.

The Library collection 'Letters to A.L. Smith' contains a substantial group concerning W.E.A. matters,1916-1920.

15. Vacation Reading Parties

There are a number of files etc. concerning F.F. Urquhart's Chalet (Chalet des Mélèzes, near S. Germain, Haute Savoie, France)[26] and the Mount, Churchill, Oxon both of which were venues for reading parties: 20th century.

16. The Balliol College Record

The College has circulated an annual magazine containing College news of all kinds to old members almost every year since 1910.

III THE PRESENT ARRANGEMENT AND EXTENT OF THE ARCHIVES

The books and papers in the Archives are arranged in the following groups, which are, however, purely nominal - material on most matters is distributed between several groups in a hopelessly inconsistent manner because the arrangement has evolved under the influence of the thinking and interests of several departments and people over more than a hundred years. The organisation within the groups often appears illogical as well.

Statutes
16th-20th centuries ca. 10 items

Government
16th-20th centuries ca. 40 items

Formal Archives
12th-20th centuries ca. 6000 items

Estates
16th-20 centuries ca. 60 items

Patronage Papers
19th-20th centuries ca. 60 items

Additional Patronage Papers
19th-20th centuries 3 items

Membership
16th-20th centuries ca. 2000 items

Bursars' Books Series I
16th-20th centuries ca. 600 items

Bursars' Books Series II
19th-20th centuries ca. 400 items

Miscellaneous Bursary Papers
18th-20th centuries ca. 300 items

Miscellaneous College Office Papers
20th century ca. 50 items

BALLIOL COLLEGE ARCHIVES

Buildings
18th-20th centuries ca. 50 items

Departments
17th-20th centuries ca. 100 items

Benefactions
17th-20th centuries ca. 10 items

Plate
16th-20th centuries ca. 40 items

Scholarships and Exhibitions
18th-20th centuries ca. 15 items

Studies and Discipline
19th-20th centuries ca. 10 items

Sport
19th-20th centuries ca. 50 items

Societies
19th-20th centuries ca. 50 items

Junior Common Room
20th century ca. 100 items

Photographs
19th-20th centuries ca. 50 items

General Miscellany
19th-20th centuries ca. 50 items

In the above summary an 'item' is anything which is individually listed - it might be anything from a single sheet to a massive ledger or box of papers. There are well over 10,000 items in the whole collection. About half of these are single documents, rather more than 1000 are volumes, the remainder mostly being bundles or files. Such files themselves often contain a hundred or more documents which are not listed separately.

IV AIDS TO ARCHIVES SEARCHERS

A LISTS

A complete list of the collection, as it lies in the arrangement outlined in Section III, has been made. A separate list, giving fuller detail in some cases, exists for the Formal Archives.

B INDEXES

The complete list is indexed, but only on a selective basis; the Formal Archives list is indexed more fully. The Lease Books are indexed. A card index to the principal College Minute Books from about 1925 is kept up to date as a current working tool by the Bursary. The Admissions Book for 1636-1682 is indexed. Admissions 1682-1833 are not, but the printed Registers[1] which begin in 1833 are. An index in the Bodleian Library compiled by Clark[2] gives all the members 1518-1893 he could identify, in a single alphabetical sequence. It is important to note that Foster's 'Alumni Oxonienses'[3] was compiled largely from University records and thus often misses altogether members of the College who never matriculated (non-matriculation was common in the 16th and 17th centuries, running as high as 25% at some periods) and attributes to other Colleges members who migrated to or from Balliol without this being noticed in University records - inter-college migration was more frequent up to the last century than it is now.

C ABSTRACTS AND TRANSCRIPTS

Abstracts and transcripts of most of the early (i.e. pre-1500) deeds in the Formal Archives are available. Transcripts of the Admissions Books 1636-1833 and of the English Register 1794-1875 have been made.

D PHOTOGRAPHS AND MICROFILMS

Photographs have been taken of all Statutes, Foundation Deeds and Charters and also of all significant Estates Maps. The Latin and English Registers have been microfilmed from the earliest available dates to the present. Further microfilming, especially of the accounts, is planned.

BALLIOL COLLEGE ARCHIVES

Volumes should be cited with a brief description and date. All other items can be cited simply by the name of the series in which they are listed (Formal Archives, Miscellaneous Bursary Papers etc.) and the appropriate number or code on the item or its box - but a brief description is helpful with these as well. Two particularly complicated confusions are found in connection with references to the Formal Archives. All items in this series were coded in the nineteenth century with a capital letter (originally designating a cabinet) a number (designating a drawer) and another number (for the item itself) - e.g. A.23.12 would be the twelfth item in the twenty-third drawer of the first cabinet. There are a number of cases where the same number was used twice in error. More seriously, exactly the same system of letters and numbers had previously been used for the Library pressmarks for early printed books and manuscripts, which were, to complete the confusion, referred to at that time as Archives. Without a word or two of description a citation in the form e.g. Arch. A.23.12 is therefore utterly ambiguous and could mean either an early printed book or an item in the Formal Archives.

V SOURCES IN THE COLLEGE LIBRARY

All the material which is briefly surveyed here is in the custody of the Librarian, to whom applications for access should be addressed.

A LIBRARY RECORDS

The pre-1900 Library records include the following:

1. Catalogues

Of printed works:

Several catalogues and working lists, n.d. but all of 1600-1750.

A catalogue of books associated with Sir Thomas Wendy, 1673.

A catalogue dated 1709.

A catalogue apparently dated 1721 - but this date may be a mere doodle, and this catalogue is possibly earlier than that of 1709.

An annotated Bodleian Library Catalogue of 1738, 4 volumes.

A catalogue, n.d., ca. 1800, probably made during the Library reorganisation which was completed in 1799.

An annotated Bodleian Library Catalogue of 1843-1851, 6 volumes.

The Library Catalogue was printed in 1871:[1] there is a manuscript supplement "complete down to 1 May 1874".

Of manuscripts:

A catalogue, 1762.

A catalogue, n.d., of the late 18th century, with later amendments.

2. Benefaction book

One volume, beginning with a list of early gifts to the Library in a 17th century hand; gifts up to 1839 are recorded.

3. Loan registers

For the Main (i.e. Fellows') Library: 1799-1877 in 3 volumes, which also have Library Rules entered in them. Loan records 1693-1706 and 1710-1712 are to be found in one of the early catalogues.

For the Undergraduates' Library: 1871-1878.

4. Accounts

There are no separate records of Library expenditure before 1694 but the early Bursars' Books have occasional entries for chains and the writing of catalogues - not books, as accessions were probably almost entirely by gift. Two 'Deans' Books' give accounts annually concerning the Fellows' Library and the Undergraduates' Library[2], 1694-1810. There are also accounts for 1851-1891.

B. PRINTED BOOKS

The Library has an extensive collection of biographies and autobiographies of members which is a rich source of detail about the social life and personalities of the College, especially 1830-1940.

C. MANUSCRIPTS

In 1963, R.A.B. Mynors published[3] a detailed catalogue of the manuscripts then in the Library. The main concern of this scholarly work is with the College's greatest treasure: the mediaeval collection which survives from the pre-reformation

Library. These manuscripts have no archival content in themselves although the donation and pledging inscriptions they often bear are an important source for the names of early Fellows. Some of the items described by Mynors, however, have contents relevant to our present purpose, and a very substantial amount of material which is at least partly to do with the history of the College has entered the manuscript collection since his Catalogue was published. In the list of the most substantial items and groups of papers which follows, a reference such as MS 100 indicates that a description is given by Mynors: the other cases are so far not fully catalogued, although preliminary lists and descriptions are available in some cases.

1. MS 355. The Diary of Nicholas Crouch

The diary of Nicholas Crouch (Fellow 1640-1690) for the years 1634-1672. The entries are few and mostly cryptic: some College accounts for 1634-1689 are entered at the end of the volume.

2. MS 400. Liber Statutorum Collegii de Baliolo

A Statute Book written in the early 17th century, with additional entries concerning College livings.

3. MS 408. The Autobiography of Frederick Oakeley

Oakeley, a prominent figure in the Oxford Movement, was a Fellow 1827-1845.

4. MS 429. Balliofergus Drafts

Drafts and notes made by Henry Savage (Master 1650-1672) for 'Balliofergus',[4] a history of the College.

5. MS 445. The Diary of Ernest Walker

Walker was admitted as a Commoner of the College in 1887. The diary, in 7 volumes, is for the years 1888-1894.

6. The Diary of Jeremiah Milles

Milles was a Fellow 1696-1705. The diary runs from 1 Jan. 1700/1 to 26 June 1703, and consists of 30 leaves written on both sides.

7. The Jenkyns Papers

This very extensive deposited collection of Jenkyns family papers contains, among much else of genealogical and historical interest, three large boxes of papers associated with Richard Jenkyns[5] (Fellow 1803-1819, Master 1819-1854). These include the following:

Papers concerning the controversy provoked by A.W.N. Pugin's rebuilding proposals, 1843.[6]

Correspondence concerning Jenkyns' appointment as Dean of Wells, with letters of congratulation, 1845.

Letters to Jenkyns by Robert Scott (Fellow 1835-1840, Master 1854-1870), 1840-1850.

Letters of condolence to Mrs. Jenkyns, 1854.

A notebook written in Jenkyns' hand, 'Memoranda Respecting Rooms, Applicants for Admission': begins with a detailed rooms list 1818-1820 and continues with a list of men awaiting admission with parental details etc. 1816-1825.

Papers concerning the affairs and estate of George Powell (Fellow 1786-1830).

Correspondence with Matthew Baillie and William Owen about a portrait of the former by the latter, 1823.

A notebook recording Scholarship exercises 1806-1851 with printed examination papers of 1839, 1842 and n.d.

Papers and correspondence concerning the case of William George Ward,[7] (Fellow 1834-1845), 1844-1845.

8. The Scott Papers

A modest collection of letters on College business written to Robert Scott during his Mastership 1854-1870, with substantial fragments of the letter books in which he recorded his replies.

9. Jowett Material

The extensive material relating to Benjamin Jowett (Fellow 1838-1870, Master 1870-1893) in the Library is in four groups:

(a) Jowett Papers. These comprise the core of the collection used by Faber[8] for his biography. They were also used by Abbott and Campbell.[9]

(b) Jowett-Nightingale Letters. Jowett's letters to Florence Nightingale. Used by Faber and (without naming the recipient) by Abbott and Campbell.

(c) Additional Jowett Papers. These appear to have passed through the hands of Abbott and Campbell but were not seen by Faber.

(d) Miscellaneous Jowett Letters. These are letters acquired at various times by gift or purchase: they were mostly unknown to Abbott and Campbell and also to Faber.

10. The Conroy Papers

This collection comprises about thirty boxes of papers and other items associated with the 1st, 2nd and 3rd Baronets Conroy. The 3rd Baronet, Sir John Conroy FRS, was a Fellow 1890-1900. It appears that he kept and filed practically every scrap of paper which came into his hands, and also always made a copy or summary of his replies to letters. His correspondence concerns his scientific work, the Balliol-Trinity Laboratories, his pupils and all manner of Balliol affairs. Of particular interest is a bundle to do with the death of Benjamin Jowett and the controversial election of Edward Caird to succeed him as Master, 1893.[10]

11. The Palmer Papers

A small collection of letters, Balliol printed ephemera etc. from the papers of Edwin James Palmer, (Fellow 1891-1908).

12. The Caird Papers

Letters written to Edward Caird (Master 1893-1907) and related papers. 3 small boxes.

13. The Strachan Davidson Papers

Several boxes of the papers of J.L. Strachan Davidson[11] (Fellow 1866-1907, Master 1907-1916) including in the region of 500 letters of congratulation on his election as Master and his diary 1896-1912 in 7 volumes.

14. The Hartley Papers

Most of the papers of Sir Harold Hartley FRS (Fellow 1901-1941) are at Churchill College Cambridge, but there is a box of letters and papers, mostly of 1924-1930.

15. A.L. Smith Material

This is in two groups:

(a) A.L. Smith Papers. Some 50 boxes, of which one contains letters and papers of Smith (Fellow 1882-1916, Master 1916-1924) on Balliol matters 1904-1922.

(b) Letters to A.L. Smith. A few thousand letters written to Smith during his Mastership.

16. The K.N. Bell Papers

Some papers of K.N. Bell (Fellow 1919-1941), including tutorial notes on his pupils 1919-1932, with gaps.

17. Hindmarsh Manuscripts

About 1950 L.K. Hindmarsh (Balliol 1897) made extensive collections of material, a good deal of which he digested into drafts apparently intended for publication, concerning Balliol Benefactors (especially Sir Thomas Wendy); the Heraldry (mainly of Benefactors) with which the buildings, fittings, and glass are liberally adorned; and the subjects of the Portraits then in the Hall.

APPENDIX A

VISITORS

The office of Visitor was first clearly defined by new Statutes, which gave the College the unique privilege of electing its own Visitor, in 1507. From that year until the election of Richard Busby in 1691, however, the Bishops of Lincoln were generally Visitors (but not invariably - e.g. Laurence Stubbs[1] was Visitor in 1531).

1691 Richard Busby, Headmaster of Westminster school

1695 Henry Compton, Bishop of London

1713 John Robinson, Bishop of London

1723 The Hon. and Rev. Henry Brydges

1728 The Rev. Sir John Dolben, Bt.

1755 The Rev. Sir William Bunbury, Bt.

1764 Robert Hay Drummond, Archbishop of York

1777 Frederick Cornwallis, Archbishop of Canterbury

1783 John Moore, Archbishop of Canterbury

1805 Shute Barrington, Bishop of Durham

1826 William Howley, Bishop of London and Archbishop of Canterbury

1848 John Kaye, Bishop of Lincoln

1853 John Jackson, Bishop of Lincoln and of London

1885 Charles Synge Christopher Bowen, Baron Bowen of Colwood

1894 Arthur Wellesley Peel, 1st Viscount Peel

1912 Robert Threshie Reed, 1st Earl Loreburn

1923 Edward Grey, 1st Viscount Grey of Falloden

1933 Robert Younger, 1st Baron Blanesburgh of Alloa

1946 Herbert Louis Samuel, 1st Viscount Samuel of Mount Carmel

1957 Walter Turner Monckton, 1st Viscount Monckton of Brenchley

1965 Colin Hargreaves Pearson, Baron Pearson of Minnedosa

1974 Charles James Dalrymple Shaw, Baron Kilbrandon

APPENDIX B

MASTERS

The succession can be given with certainty of completeness only from the admission of Thomas Cisson in 1511. A precise contemporary record of his admission and of all his successors exists. His predecessors, on the other hand, are mostly known to us only by their chance appearances in deeds and in the records of other bodies. The list which follows is more complete than any previously printed but may still lack a few names.

Walter de Fodringeye, in 1284, 1292

Hugh de Warkenby, in 1295

Stephen of Cornwall, in 1307

Thomas de Waldeby, in 1321

Henry de Seton, in 1324

Nicholas de Luceby, in 1328

Richard de Chikwelle, in 1329

John de Poklyngton, in 1332, 1337

Hugh de Corbrigge, in 1340, 1345

William de Kyrneshale, in 1349

John Wycliffe, in 1360, 1361

John Hugate, in 1366

Thomas Tyrwhit, in 1379, 1395

Hamond Askham, in 1397

William Lambert, in 1407

Thomas Chace, in 1411, 1416

Robert Burley, in 1423, 1427

Richard Stapilton, in 1428, 1429

William Brandon, in 1440, 1441

Robert Thwaytes, in 1450, 1456

William Lambton, in 1458, 1465

John Segden, in 1469, 1475

Robert Abdy, in 1481, 1483

William Bell, in 1484, 1495

Richard Barnyngham, in 1496, 1511

Thomas Cisson, 1512-1518

Richard Stubbs, 1518-1525

William Whyte, 1525-1539

George Cotes, 1539-1545

William Wright, 1545-1547 and 1555-1559

James Brookes, 1547-1555

Francis Babington, 1559-1560

Anthony Garnet, 1560-1563

Robert Hooper, 1563-1570

John Pierse, 1570-1571

Adam Squier, 1571-1580

Edmund Lilly, 1580-1610

Robert Abbott, 1610-1616

John Parkhurst, 1617-1637

Thomas Laurence, 1637-1648

George Bradshaw, 1648-1651

Henry Savage, 1651-1672

Thomas Goode, 1672-1678

John Venn, 1678-1687

Roger Mander, 1687-1704

John Baron, 1705-1722

Joseph Hunt, 1722-1726

Theophilus Leigh, 1726-1785

John Davey, 1785-1798

John Parsons, 1798-1819

Richard Jenkyns, 1819-1854

Robert Scott, 1854-1870

Benjamin Jowett, 1870-1893

Edward Caird, 1893-1907

James Leigh Strachan Davidson, 1907-1916

Arthur Lionel Smith, 1916-1924

Alexander Dunlop Lindsay, 1924-1949

David Lindsay Keir, 1949-1966

John Edward Christopher Hill, 1966-1978

Anthony John Patrick Kenny, 1978-

Robert de Derby is given as Master in 1356 by de Paravicini,[1] and this is followed by H W C Davis[2] but the Victoria County History[3] and the revision of H W C Davis' work by R H C Davis and R Hunt[4] drop Derby's name without comment. The present writer cannot trace any authority for including him.

APPENDIX C

MAJOR BENEFACTORS

Over the centuries the College has benefited from the generosity of Benefactors far too numerous to list in full (numbered in thousands if contributors to Appeals are included) - see II.E and II.G. The principal names are recited in the Bidding Prayer:

THE BIDDING PRAYER

We render most humble and hearty thanks unto Thee, O Eternal and Heavenly Father, for all Thy Gifts and Graces most bountifully and mercifully bestowed upon us; and, namely, for Thy Benefits, our Exhibitions and Maintenance here at the Study of Virtue and good Learning, by the Liberality of JOHN BALLIOL and DEVORGUILLA his Wife, Founders of this College; Sir Philip Somervyle, Sir William Felton, William Gray Bishop of Ely, Mr. Peter Blundell, the Lady Elizabeth Periham, Dr. John Bell Bishop of Worcester, Dr. John Warner Bishop of Rochester, Sir Thomas Wendy, Dr. Richard Busby, John Snell Esquire, Dr. Henry Compton and Dr. John Robinson, successive Bishops of London, The Reverend Henry Fisher, The Reverend Thomas Williams and Jane his wife, Dr. Richard Prosser, Dr. Richard Jenkyns Master of this College, Miss Hannah Brackenbury, Francis Charles Hastings Duke of Bedford, the Reverend Benjamin Jowett Master of this College, Sir John Conroy, James Leigh Strachan Davidson Master of this College, Thomas Allnutt Earl Brassey, William Lambert Newman, Kenneth Edelman Chalmers, James Hozier Baron Newlands, Gerard Henry Craig-Sellar, Mrs. Charlotte Byron Green, Francis Fortescue Urquhart, Andrew Cecil Bradley, Oliver Gatty, Percy Hide and Ann his wife, Vivian Bulkeley-Johnson, James Westlake Platt, The Reverend Dr. John Stewart MacArthur, Harold Greville Smith, and others our Pious Benefactors: most humbly beseeching Thee to give us Grace so to use them, as may make most for our Furtherance in Virtue, and Increase in Learning, for the Comfort and Salvation of our own Souls, and the Benefit and Edification of our Brethren, and, above all, for the Glory of Thy Holy Name, through Jesus Christ our Lord and Saviour. Amen.

APPENDIX D

SPECIAL FELLOWSHIPS, SCHOLARSHIPS, EXHIBITIONS, AND PRIZES

The principal special Fellowships, Scholarships, Exhibitions and Prizes established up to 1967 are listed below, with their dates of foundation. They are not all current as there has been some consolidation, chiefly in the 19th century following reforms which diminished local preferences.

Andrew Bradley Fellowship 1936

Anderson Mauritian Scholarship 1951

Anderson French Scholarship 1952

Anderson Norwegian Scholarship 1953

Anthony Maurice Goldsmith Scholarship 1944

Arthur Higgs Scholarship 1920

Arthur James Richmond Paton Scholarship 1946

A.L. Smith Memorial Fellowship in History 1925

A.L.Smith Memorial Scholarship 1925

Bedford Lecturership 1882

Bell Exhibitions 1558

Billmeir Fellowship 1965

Blagden Exhibitions 1696

Blanesburgh Fellowship 1962

Blundell Fellowships and Scholarships 1676

Brackenbury Scholarship 1866

Brassey Scholarship 1918

Browne Exhibitions 1586

Busby Lecturership 17th century

Charles Elton Exhibition 1914

Craig-Sellar Fellowship 1931

Dale-Plender Scholarship 1955

Deakin Scholarship 1949

Duncan Campbell Macgregor Fellowship 1941

Dunch Exhibition 1605

Dyson Research Fellowship in Greek Studies 1960

Edgcombe Exhibitions 18th century

Edward Maurice Hill Scholarship 1952

Ellsworth Exhibitions 1714

Eric Raymond Noble Scholarships 1948

Ernest Walker Prize 1949

Fairfax Fellowship in Philosophy 1963

Fawkes Memorial Fellowship and Scholarship 1946

Felix Frankfurter Memorial Fellowship in Law 1966

George Paddison and Lothian Stevens Exhibition 1923

Greaves Exhibition, 17th century

Guinness Scholarship, 20th century

Harris Exhibitions 1713

Headlam Exhibitions 1725

Herbert Samuel Fellowship in Philosophy 1964

Herbertson Prize 1919

Holmes Scholarship in Music 1955

James Gay Exhibition 1943

James Hall Prize 1911

Jasper Ridley Prize 1945

Jenkyns Exhibition 1850

John Ewan Frazer Scholarship 1930

Jowett Lecturerships 1893

Jowett Fellowships 1907

Jowett Exhibition in Natural Science 20th century

J.H. Hofmeyr Fellowship 1964

Keith Rae Exhibition 1917

Kington-Oliphant Prize 1902

Lazarus Fletcher Scholarship 1951

Lewis Masefield Studentship 1943

Lewis Nettleship Memorial Scholarship 1894

Lord Thomson of Fleet Fellowship in Economics 1965

Mander Exhibitions 1704

Maurice Lubbock Scholarship in Engineering 1958

Mouat Jones Scholarship in Natural Science 1954

Newlands Scholarship 1908

Newman Exhibition 1923

Newte Exhibitions 1715

Oliver Gatty Fellowship 1933

Periam Fellowships and Scholarships 1620

Powell Prize 1830

Prosser Exhibitions 1839

Radcliffe-Henry Skynner Research Fellowship 1963

Reynolds Scholarship 1951

Robert Younger Prize 1926

Robert Sebag-Montefiore Scholarship 1916

Robert Maxwell Fellowship in Politics 1965

Robin Hollway Scholarship 1921 and 1955

Roger Hall Prize 1919

Sir Raymond Beazley Essay Prize 1966

Sir William Markby Scholarship 1929

Sir Francis Fremantle Lectureship 1944

Snell Exhibitions 1699

Spring-Rice Memorial Travelling Scholarships 1926

S.S. Clarke Memorial Exhibition 1925

The Raja Sir Maharaj Singh Prize 20th century

Vincent Massey Fellowship 1932

Walter Galpin Scholarship 1936

Warner Exhibitions 17th century

Williams Exhibitions 1830

Wycliffe Prize 1925

APPENDIX E

WILLS

The Archives, especially the Formal Archives, contain numerous copies and extracts of wills. Those which are individually numbered are listed below. There is often confusion over the date, which may be that of the will, of its probate or that of the copy. A number of the early ones are printed by Salter.[1] The list is by no means exhaustive. There are many files (see IIE, IIG and Appendix D) relating to bequests and endowments which are likely to contain further wills or extracts and a number of will extracts are entered in the Latin and English Registers, the books of some Trust Funds etc.

Awdley, Sir Thomas 1544

Baron, John 1722

Binne, John of Oxford 1304 (see Salter)

Biryton, John of Cobcote Oxon 1578

Blagdon, Edward of Washfield Devon 1675

Blake, Peter of Andover 1693

Blundell, Peter 1599

Bocke, John 1382 (see Salter)

Boutle, Simon of Tendring 1682

Branthwaite, Richard of St. Giles, Oxford 1645

Bush, James 1830

Bush, The Rev. James 1849

Chislamtone, Robert of Oxford 1415 (see Salter)

Chyslamtone, William 1398 (see Salter)

Coleston, Henry 1796

Conroy, Sir John 1900

Davey, John 1798

Deeke, Thomas 1759

Dendy, Capt. Ralph 1917

Devyn, John of Henley on Thames 1470

Ellsworth, Richard, sen., of Bickham, Somerset 1701

Ellsworth, Rich, jun. 1715

Fensham, John 1758

Finch, The Rev. Robert 1830

Fouke, John of 1326 (see Salter)

Goldsmith, A.M. 1942

Harris, Charles of Oxford 1713

Hide, Mrs. E.A. 1938

Hide, Percy 1938

Hitchings, Sir Edward 1835

Hunt, Joseph 1726

Hurst, Augusta 1734

Jenkyns, Dr. Richard 1854

Jowett, The Rev. Benjamin 1893

Lancaster, Sir James of London 1618

Leigh, Theophilus 1785

Mander, Roger 1704

More, John of Glaseley, Salop 1672

Oliver, Joseph 1744

Overhee, Isolda wife of Richard 1307 (see Salter)

Peacock, The Rev. W.G. 1937

Pearson, John 1611

Phelps, Samuel, sen., of Badingshaw, London 1672

Powell, The Rev. George 1830

Prosser, Dr. Richard 1828

Robinson, Elizabeth of Brackenthwaite 1587

Robinson, John 1810

Sandys, William Lord 1668

Saucer, John le of Oxford 1339 (see Salter)

Scott, Mrs. Sarah 1750

Skynner, Henry 1879

Snell, John of Ufton, Warwicks 1679

Spencer, Mrs. Anne of Harbury, Warwicks 1651

Urquhart, F.F. 1934

Venn, John 1687

Virley, Robert the elder 1813

Ward, Richard 1647

White, Francis 1716

Whitworth, R.S.H. 1823

Whitworth, Rev. William 1802

Wight, Rev. John of Tetbury 1774

Williams, Jane of Bere Regis 1831

Woodward, Miss Mary 1884

APPENDIX F

SEALS

The seals attached to documents in the Formal Archives are mostly not described (notable exceptions covered by Salter[1] are the seal of Dervorguilla Lady of Balliol, the effective Foundress, 1282; early seals of the College, the University and the Chancellor; the seal of Queen Margaret, 1314) but a brief survey and almost complete photographic record of the Great Seals has been made. There are examples of Edward I, II, III, IV, VI; Elizabeth I; Henry III, VI, VIII; James I; Richard II, III; Victoria.

BALLIOL COLLEGE ARCHIVES

NOTES

SECTION I

1. The best concise account of the history of the College is in 'The Victoria History of the Counties of England', Oxfordshire, III, p82. A more popular illustrated account is available: 'Balliol College Oxford. A Brief History and Guide', 1982.

2. Pages 68 and 80. Quoted as translated by de Paravicini[3] with some slips corrected.

3. F. de Paravicini 'Early History of Balliol College', 1891.

4. Bursars' Book I.E.1.

5. A. Clark 'The Life and Times of Anthony Wood', II (1892), p45.

6. Lease Log-book; see H.E. Salter, 'Oxford Balliol Deeds', 1913, p345.

7. F.W. Steer 'The Archives of New College, Oxford', 1974, p46: New College Archives 2437.

8. 'Fourth Report of the Royal Commission on Historical Manuscripts', 1874.

9. A. Clark, Bodleian MS.Top.Oxon. e. 123/1.

10. A. Wood 'Athenae Oxonienses', 1721, II p499.

SECTION II

1. H.E. Salter 'Oxford Balliol Deeds', 1913.

2. F. de Paravicini 'Early History of Balliol College', 1891.

BALLIOL COLLEGE ARCHIVES

3. Anonymous (Sir John Conroy) 'Domus de Balliolo', n.d. about 1891.

4. A.B. Emden 'A Biographical Register of the University of Oxford to AD 1500', 1957-9, and 'A Biographical Register of the University of Oxford AD 1501 to 1540', 1974.

5. 'Balliol College Register' in five editions: 1832-1914 (1914), 1833-1933 (1934), 1900-1950 (1953), 1916-1967 (1969) and 1930-1980 (1983).

6. (a) 'Balliol College War Memorial Book', 1924, 2 volumes. See also 'Balliol's "Lost Generation"', Balliol College Record, 1975.

   (b) W.I. Addison 'The Snell Exhibitions from the University of Glasgow to Balliol College Oxford', 1901.

7. A.B. Emden 'The Last Pre-Reformation Rotulus Benefactorum and List of Obits of Balliol College', Balliol College Record (supplement), 1967.

8. F.L.M. Willis-Bund, Appendix II, in 'A History of Balliol College' by H.W.C. Davis, revised by R.H.C. Davis and R. Hunt, 1963.

9. C. M. Barron 'The Medieval Guildhall of London ', 1974.

10. E.B. Fryde and J.R.L. Highfield 'An Oxfordshire Deed of Balliol College', Oxoniensia, 1955, XX, 40.

11. A. Clark 'Essex and Balliol College', The Essex Review, Jan 1912; see also 'The Essex Livings', Balliol College Record, 1966.

12. J. Sherwood and N. Pevsner 'The Buildings of England: Oxfordshire', 1974.

13. 'The Victoria History of the Counties of England', Oxfordshire, III, p95.

14. Bodleian MS.Top.Oxon. a. 23(R).

15. J.N. Bryson, 'The Balliol that might have been. Pugin's rejected designs.' Country Life, 27 June 1963.

16. Bodleian MS.Top. Oxon. e. 124/9-10

17. V.H.H. Green 'The Commonwealth of Lincoln College 1427-1977', 1979.

18. T.W.M. Smith 'The Balliol Trinity Laboratories', in 'Balliol Studies' ed. J.M. Prest, 1982.

19. V.H. Galbraith 'A Memorandum of Holywell Manor', 1937.

20. Mrs. R.L. Poole 'Catalogue of Portraits in the Possession of the University, Colleges, City and County of Oxford', 1925.

21. R. McCormmack 'The Atomic Theory of John William Nicholson', Archive for History of the Exact Sciences, 1966, 3, 160.

22. R. Crawford 'T.S. Eliot, A.D. Lindsay and N.M. Iovetz-Tereschenko' Balliol College Record, 1983.

23. R. Lister 'College Stamps of Oxford and Cambridge', 1966.

24. C. Bailey 'A Short History of the Balliol Boys' Club 1907-1950', 1950.

25. D. Scott 'A.D. Lindsay. A Biography', 1971, Ch.4.

26. C. Bailey, 'Francis Fortescue Urquhart. A Memoir', 1936. Appendix I is a list of those attending Chalet Parties 1891-1931.

SECTION IV

1. 'Balliol College Register' in five editions: 1832-1914 (1914), 1833-1933 (1934), 1900-1950 (1953), 1916-1967 (1969) and 1930-1980 (1983).

2. A. Clark, Bodleian MS.Top.Oxon. e. 96-106.

3. J. Foster 'Alumni Oxonienses 1500-1714', 1891, and 'Alumni Oxonienses 1715-1886', 1887.

SECTION V

1. 'Catalogue of Printed Books in Balliol College Library', 1871.

2. 'Eighteenth-century Balliol. (ii) The Eighteenth-century Undergraduates' Library', Balliol College Record, 1980.

3. R.A.B. Mynors 'Catalogue of the Manuscripts of Balliol College, Oxford', 1963.

4. H. Savage 'Balliofergus', 1668.

5. They were much used in connection with 'Sound Religion and Useful Learning', in 'Balliol Studies' ed. J.M. Prest, 1982.

6. 'The Civil War of 1843', Balliol College Record, 1978.

7. W. Ward 'William George Ward and the Oxford Movement', 1889.

8. G. Faber 'Jowett', 1957.

9. E. Abbott and L. Campbell 'The Life and Letters of Benjamin Jowett', 1897.

10. 'A Contested Mastership. The Election of Jowett's Successor', Balliol College Record, 1977.

11. J.W. Mackail 'James Leigh Strachan Davidson', 1925.

APPENDIX A

1. This exception is overlooked in the Victoria County History[2] and wrongly given as Richard Stubbs by Davis.[3] There were also times when external dignitaries intruded and exercised Visitor-like authority.

2. 'The Victoria History of the Counties of England', Oxfordshire, III, p95.

3. H.W.C. Davis 'A History of Balliol College', 1899.

APPENDIX B

1. F. de Paravicini 'Early History of Balliol College', 1891.

2. H.W.C. Davis 'A History of Balliol College',1899.

3. 'The Victoria History of the Counties of England', Oxfordshire, III, p95.

4. H.W.C. Davis 'A History of Balliol College', revised by R.H.C. Davis and R. Hunt, 1963.

APPENDIX E

1. H.E. Salter 'Oxford Balliol Deeds',1913.

APPENDIX F

1. H.E.Salter 'Oxford Balliol Deeds',1913.

INDEX